10 PERSONAL SKILLS FOR YOUR CAREER SUCCESS

Essential skills to excel in your career and business
Become a high-performing person
Stand out early in your career
Be promoted more quickly than your peers

By Enock A. Ebbah

10

PERSONAL SKILLS FOR YOUR CAREER SUCCESS

I dedicate this book to my mother, Tanti Vic, for making me informed of the essence and the impact of my early childhood behaviours.

Contents

INTRODUCTION

Early in my career, I observed that certain people who showed a distinct set of behaviours were likely to be promoted and had a fulfilling career right from the outset. I grew up in a rural area; however, I had to leave for the city to study at college and university in my teenage years. It was challenging not knowing anyone in college, where there were more than 2,000 students. Surviving meant learning to fit it. There is a stigma attached to being from a rural area, and people think you have weird behaviours and manners. This meant that, from the very outset, I had to observe the behaviours of other students from the cities to ensure that I did not stand out in the wrong way. Indeed, I would watch the actions of the house prefects and head boys over the years. I paid attention to the behaviour of the people who were most likely to be promoted to such positions. That early teenage experience convinced me that it was no coincidence that certain people got promoted – it was due to their behaviour.

My experiences in various sectors, from the oil and gas industry to the military, to academia, taught me that one must exhibit a set of life skills to stand out, be promoted, and reap a successful career from the outset. No doubt this is the case in other sectors too.

However, I am amazed that there is a greater emphasis on training college and university graduates to secure a job or get into a dream career, rather than succeed in one. In my experience, working with young people in charities and academia, there is little focus on the primary life skills they need to succeed in their careers. Let us say that a company employs 20 people in a graduate development program. In two years, the company needs to promote three people because there are internal opportunities available. Who do you think is most likely to be promoted? You've guessed it, it's those who exhibit the necessary life skills who stand the best chance.

What follows are my 10 life skills that will help you demonstrate behaviours to get ahead and stand out from your peers early on in your career. These life skills are not secret or set in stone. They are based on my observations of the behaviours of work colleagues who have succeeded in their careers. They are designed to help you stand out from the crowd and beat the competition for the best promotions and achievements in your workplace. These life skills are not a revelation, but rather reminders that generate results. Use them to impact your workplace and leave a lasting, positive impression so you can excel in your career or business.

I'd love to hear how you get on or if you have any tips to share. If the 10 life skills make a difference to you or someone you know, I am always interested in hearing from you. You can email me at Enock@ebbahsustainovation.co.

Enock Ebbah

Chapter 1: RESILIENCE

"It is not the strongest of the species that survive, nor the most intelligent, but the most **resilient** and responsive to change."

— Charles Darwin

Resilient people develop a mental capacity to recover quickly from difficulties and adversities. From the Latin origin, resilience means the act "to rebound, recoil." Resilient people possess the ability to recoil, not just back into their original shape, but to recover so they are even more robust, wiser, and better than before. So, how do you usually respond to adversity and life difficulties? Do you blame yourself or other people for what is happening to you? Do you ask why this could happen to me, or do you face adversity with a mental attitude that you can, and will, rebound from this even better and stronger?

Like most people in life, I have had my fair share of adversity and grappled with getting out of it better and stronger. Until the age of 15, I did not experience hardship and difficulties growing up in Ghana as it developed. I count myself lucky because I was in a small minority. Unfortunately, most of the kids I grew up with, in my school and neighbourhood, had different stories. I remember vividly that my best friend, George, walked eight kilometres every day from home to school and back again, even as young as eight years old. I felt so much empathy for him that I convinced my parents to let him live with us until he finished secondary school. To date, anytime I talk to George, he exhibits a mental capacity to take any challenges that he faces in his stride, enabling him to manage his business successfully. Even with my military experience, I find it challenging to keep up with his pace when I take a walk with him each time I pay a visit.

Apart from my friend George's example, I have seen abject poverty in my childhood neighbourhood: babies exposed to excessive dust released from stones being cracked by their mothers to make a living. These scenes remain vivid in my memory. At the age of 14, some of my classmates went to a farm to gather food before they started school. No wonder these students dozed off in class many times. Some children in my neighbourhood could not even go to school because their parents could not afford the fees.

I had my first memorable taste of distress when I left home for the first time at 15 for a college of more than 2,000 students, not knowing a single one. It was daunting because, for the first time, I had left my parents and the familiar environment of home, for a new place where I had to learn how to make friends and survive. The first year in male-only colleges in Ghana at the time, in 2000 was notorious for bullying, or character building, whichever you may choose to call it. I had to learn to survive. That was the first time I can remember having to dig deep to develop a mental capacity for distress and to live out of my comfort zone.

Many years later, in mid-2007, I travelled to Great Britain. Again, I knew no one that I could count on in such a big and great country. I made friends who could rely on an extended family for support. Initially, I found it challenging to find work because I had no work experience until I enlisted in the British Army in early 2008 as a military vehicle mechanic. Then, I pursued postgraduate study to retrain as a project engineer in the gas industry. I have faced many professional and personal failures and rejections along the way, and still do. I had to exhibit the art of resilience to endure the pain of losing on the way to success and to recover quickly from disappointments, adversities, and failures.

Bad experiences in life can often lead to pain. Pain can cause us to freeze in our tracks and not continue towards our goal for fear of getting hurt. Or, if you are resilient, pain leads you to confront life's difficulties and make the necessary adjustments to adapt. Resilient people have a mental capacity to rebound from adversity. They can even come out the other side stronger. When faced with life's challenges, it's easy to ride along with the flow. Swimming against the tide is painful, and it takes a person with the mental strength to choose the less comfortable option.

What are the essential skills that we need to develop resilience? How can we turn bad experiences and life problems into opportunities for growth?

You are applying skills needed for improved and effective resilience in your life.

Do not try to avoid pain in your quest to achieve your goals. As John C. Maxwell puts it in his book, *The 15 Invaluable Laws of Growth*, one of which is the "law of pain," we can make the pain stop us dead in our tracks, or it can cause us to face who we are and where we are. You must pay your dues in sacrifice and pain on your way to achieving a gain. No one likes to face pain in life if they can avoid it. There is no need to meet pain if you don't have to. Facing your adversity head-on still doesn't make it easy to overcome. But it is even more difficult when you become so reluctant to face your misfortunes. Our success is hinged on how well we handle the troubles and affliction that come our way. As Warren G Lester puts it: "Success in life comes not from holding a good hand, but in playing a poor hand well." We live in a time that people are quick to expose our shortcomings, as if not everyone has them. But, when we come into the difficult times in our lives, we must see that it is only a passing season which is not here to stay. Our success is hinged on how well we play a lousy hand and make the best out of a dire situation. We should not worry about being perfect during a bad situation. Instead, we must switch to survival mode and strive to improve incrementally day-by-day to make the best out of a problem. Imagine you are fit and able, and suddenly you injure your foot. If a predator pursues you, your mind must initially switch to survival mode to ensure you do not get eaten. You then give yourself time to heal, and once you have recovered, you can then attack and fight the predator to take it out. Maintaining a positive mental attitude is vital when you are dealt a bad situation.

Practice patience. As David G. Allen notes: "Patience is the calm acceptance that things can happen in a different order than the one you have imagined." When faced with adversity, we must realize that there is power in patience. While we are waiting for things to turn around in our favour, we may be required to have the courage and strength to be silent and avoid saying something that we might regret later in life. Practicing patience is accepting that you cannot rush time; you must allow it to elapse for things to change. As Mahatma Gandhi puts it: "To lose patience is to lose the battle." It is not just about waiting, but rather how you stay. It would help if you occupied your time with meaningful activities, such as learning a new sport or musical instrument or writing a book. Staring at the clock in anticipation creates anxiety. It does not help you to cope well during a period when you are going through life challenges and overcoming adversity.

Choose the right support partners and associations. We need to carefully select family and friends who can support us as we bounce back from life difficulties. Associating with the wrong people when you are going through a crisis is a recipe for disaster. You are guaranteed to fail to recover from setbacks if you associate with corrupting influences. The challenge is that we cannot be sure that the partners who sang Hosanna with us in good times will show up for us in our difficult times. Naturally, there is a temptation to call on existing networks and associations in times of need. However, choosing to battle adversity with the wrong partners will bring you down, dampen your spirit, and cripple you with much guilt and condemnation. Remember, not everyone will join you when you are going through pain or a time of distress. So, be sure to avoid wasting your time on people who say, "We told you so," or "How could you be so stupid." You do not have time to dampen your spirit. Instead, you need a quickened soul to weather the storm. Do not be dismayed or worried about letting go of your associations that will not help you bounce back from adversity. Excellent and helpful associations sometimes feel God-sent; they just come in your time of need to get you out of your hell. The right partners will only ask questions during the crisis to gather evidence, which you can use to make informed decisions for the future and be better and wiser.

See it as an opportunity for personal growth. When we face life difficulties, it can be a unique opportunity to eliminate unhelpful behaviors. Sometimes, what brought us to where we are now will not take us forward, so losing it prompts us to find a far better replacement or new jewel. We tend to spend too much time pondering what we have lost. We miss an opportunity because we are busy covering our faces and eyes in shame, blinding us to new possibilities. See what you have lost during failure as pruning your garden for growth. You have not buried it in the ground but instead planted a seed to grow and multiply that appeared to have been lost. Accepting loss is a crucial step to letting go of guilt and the burden of condemnation because some associations are incredibly good at filling up your head. Learn to let go and practice having a positive outlook which gives you the mental capacity to overcome adversity. When you see a beautiful butterfly, remember that a caterpillar did all the hard work and bore the pain.

Be courageous enough to accept challenges from yourself and others. You must be honest and take a hard look in the mirror. Look at yourself when no one is watching. Take a good look at the hidden aspects of your life known to you but not understood by others. As Victor Frankl states: "When we are no longer able to change a situation, we are challenged to change ourselves." Face your demons head-on to make necessary changes in crucial areas of your life. To meet yourself is to know yourself and to ask: "Who am I really?" People not facing themselves is one of the fundamental reasons why they are held back from making significant progress. Society finds it easy to discuss wrongdoings, such as infidelity and theft, rather than dealing with innate sins such as gossip, lies, and subtle deceits. Note the biblical story of the prodigal son, who one day "came to himself" before making the first step towards change and redemption that allowed him to return to his father. Like the prodigal son, many people take far too many years to come to themselves, to enable change from within.

It would help if you made it a habit to challenge yourself with ongoing and regular activities that stretch you. This improves your resilience muscle. You build a continuous belief that you have the capacity and discipline to overcome difficulties. A soldier wears a medal to remind himself, or herself, that they can fight the battles in front of them. Without complacency, they can dig deep, drawing on the strength of their resilience muscle to see them through the challenges ahead. See to it that you are pursuing your purpose and passion in life. Because, yes, there will be challenges in your journey, but your passion helps make it effortless. When you enjoy what you do, your work does not become a burden. You see your career as an opportunity to practice today to get better tomorrow. You find it easier to nourish your mind. Society, family, friends, and schools must develop a curriculum that actively builds young people's resilience muscle. These exercises should be continuous from childhood, through adolescence, to adulthood. It must not necessarily stop at maturity because life challenges continue throughout one's lifetime. As George S. Patton notes: "Moral courage is the most valuable and usually the most absent characteristic in men." I agree with this statement. I find that people are unwilling to tell the truth, which will change lives for reasons I do not know or comprehend. To build resilience that can improve your life, you must be courageous and humble to listen to constructive feedback. One of the most bizarre moments in my professional career was to witness how emotional some of my colleagues became on a leadership training course. We received 360-degree feedback from work colleagues that highlighted what we were doing well and where we needed to improve and areas where those giving feedback would like to see a change. Some of the team found this difficult, even where deep down we knew it was a hard truth. We must muster the courage and be willing to be challenged.

Chapter 2: PROACTIVE

"So, each time a person decides to wait for 'time to change things,' they are waiting for other people to change their fortunes."

— Innocent Mwatsikesimbe

A proactive person creates or controls a situation in anticipation of future needs. They take responsibility for actions when required, rather than just responding after events have happened. However, a reactive person solves problems as and when they arise, which is less effective. To be proactive involves planning well in advance by taking a visionary trip into the future and completing tasks in anticipation of what could happen. So, are you proactive or reactive?

Whether you are in a place of work or study, you need to develop your personal and professional development goals. I know that my annual appraisal meeting is due sometime in December, so I start planning and preparing six weeks beforehand. I research precisely what I need to develop my career. I take responsibility for my progress. I spend time reflecting on the year: what went well, and what needs improvement or could have been done differently. It would be best if you took full responsibility for your personal and professional development. Even if you have a sponsor or mentor that supports you, you must dedicate time to plan and prepare for your personal and professional development.

How to be more proactive

Foresee potential obstacles. You must think ahead about delivering results. Thinking forward includes a thorough preview of the list of activities, hurdles, and challenges that must be overcome in the future. You must break down the final goal into several steps and examine each one meticulously. You must anticipate the challenges that you need to overcome at each precise stage. The more you can break each process into finite steps, the better the chances of unearthing potential issues when delivering a project. As an engineering project lead, I authorized a construction company to erect a scaffold for a third party to enter a vessel through a 20-inch entrance. On the day of vessel entry, the third party advised that the tripod that had been erected was not a safe enough method of entry. The lesson here was that the third party needed to have a conversation with the scaffolding company at the planning stage. I passed on the tripod's tiny detail to the scaffolding company at the project specification stage. A dedicated risk assessment document is used to record all potential hazards and safety issues that must be eliminated or reduced as reasonably as possible. There is inevitably no guarantee that this will stop every single challenge at the planning stage. Still, the goal is ongoing attempts to make improvements. It may be cost-effective to plan for standby power as an insurance policy for unexpected outages. It may be useful to spend money on standby resources if the outlay is lower than the potential cost of not having them. Make adequate contingency plans that consider all possible future situations.

Ask questions. To be proactive is to make decisions for controlling a future event. To close the gap between the expected future event and the real event, one must ask enough questions so that you can examine the response to make a meaningful decision. It is essential to ask relevant, open, and closed questions. For example: "How will you complete the building foundation?" This is an open-ended question, encouraging the one answering to talk about more than one approach that may be feasible.

On the other hand, "How long will it take to lay the building foundation?" is a closed question that requires a specific answer. As Peter Abelard once said: "The key to wisdom is this – constant and frequent questioning, for by doubting, we are led to question, by questioning we arrive at the truth." Asking the right questions allows one to understand the processes involved in completing a task. We can unearth the fundamental pieces of information that we need.

Ask for feedback. You must develop a willingness to ask for feedback from peers, colleagues, supervisors, partners, customers, and business associates. Feedback can be open-ended. The person reviewing gives a reflection on your work and advises on areas of improvement and blind spots. You must develop the capacity to act on feedback. Be willing to make the necessary changes so that you can achieve the right outcome in the future. Good feedback is constructive and offers the chance to produce better and effective results. For example, you are setting up a business, so you ran market research to gain insight into critical customer values. The greater the number and spread of respondents, the better.

Take the initiative. It may not be your role to solve that problem in your workplace. But a proactive person takes the initiative to improve processes and has a desire to make things better. Assertive people are willing to step out of their comfort zone to try new ways of improving things. Those who take the initiative do not take heed to "We have always done it this way," "This is not your/my job," "It is above my paygrade," or "We tried it years ago, and it failed." Taking the initiative is a clear sign of a proactive leader. They become explicit role models because they are willing to create a path where there isn't one. These paths can often lead to breakthroughs. It is common to see employees doing the very minimum when they turn up to work. Those who lack initiative work just to survive and get a paycheck. They lack enthusiasm, are resistant to change, and always wait to be told what to do. Conversely, when a proactive person attends a meeting and the manager fails to show at the last minute, he or she will lead the session to ensure the time is not wasted and pass on information to the manager, rather than cancel the meeting.

Chapter 3: PROBLEM-SOLVING

"All of life is a series of problems to be solved and difficulties to be overcome. Your ability to effectively solve problems is a metric for your potential to earn more as an employee and a businessperson."

— Brian Tracy

What is a problem?

The *Concise Oxford English Dictionary* defines a problem as:

"A doubtful or difficult matter requiring a solution."

And

"Something hard to understand or accomplish or deal with."

You need to consider at what point do you feel or understand that a situation is a problem? If anyone perceives that a problem exists, it must be addressed. Denying its existence is very toxic and a missed opportunity.

We all encounter problems, whether in our personal life or a professional setting. Hence, if you are going to succeed in life, you need to have the ability to solve problems. There are several steps to solving problems. Below I have identified a four-step process; however, you may prefer a more simplified or complicated approach that works alongside this book's steps. The avid reader may find it helpful to explore other measures that are peculiar to their circumstances. There is no silver bullet to solve every problem we encounter in life; otherwise, life would be too simplistic. This chapter aims to develop your ability to solve problems efficiently.

It will help if we see the journey of problem-solving as embarking on an adventure. This adventure could be setting up a new business or starting a new role with a new company. You may have work experience, but you enter new territory with unique challenges that will present unknowns. Employers look for experienced applicants because they are betting that they will use their learned expertise in solving a problem from a previous setting to solve future problems. It is expected that they can apply their problem-solving skills in the new environment. What is somewhat known is the set of problem-solving skills; the unknowns are the problems to be solved.

The problem-solving process

Applying suitable solutions to life and business problems can be accomplished by implementing the fundamental four-step problem-solving process and methodology outlined below.

Define and understand the problem

The key to defining a problem well is to diagnose the entire situation at hand and not merely look at the symptoms. You must identify the problem so that you do not end up focusing on something else. You need to understand the problem by gathering relevant information to gain a full picture of the issue. You are only as good as the information in front of you, so you need to collect relevant information about all facets of the problem to give a balanced view. Do not fall into the trap of listening to one-sided arguments and sources. Your understanding of the problem will help you to gather the right depth and breadth of information. You need good researching skills to succeed at this stage.

TIP: you need good teamwork skills and emotional intelligence to appreciate the input of others on the team.

Identify the root causes

Once you have a detailed understanding of the problem, you need to perform a root cause analysis. An essential life skill is to ask the right questions to lead you to the problem's root cause. One cannot substitute the pain symptoms with the root cause of a problem. There are several schools of thought with many tools and techniques for identifying the root cause of problems. These tools usually ask follow-up questions until you get from the top to the trunk, to the root of the problem. The business sector you work in will have its preferred root cause techniques. Examples of root cause techniques include, but are not limited to, Root Cause Analysis, Five Whys, The Four-Step Innovation Process, and The FOCUS Model.

Generate alternative solutions

Here, consider and evaluate multiple alternative solutions to the problem. Establish what the ideal solution should look like and use it to develop a roadmap for assessing alternative solutions. You must evaluate each possible solution to find the best one. Ensure the desired solution is what it *should* look like and not what we would *like* it to be.

TIP: you need creative thinking skills to succeed at this stage. It would also help if you managed risks.

Evaluate and select an alternative – with critical thinking

We are now moving from problem analysis to a method of decision-making. Evaluate any constraints on the proposed solution. Does it have cost implications that make it unviable? Some solutions look good but are not feasible to deliver. Select the solution that is practical to implement with no negative knock-on effects. Take as much time as possible to think and reflect on your proposed choice. The selected solution must be the best among the options that fit within the identified constraints set out at the beginning of the problem-solving process. Take note of any assumptions so that you can check them during the implementation stage.

TIP: you need good decision-making skills to succeed at this stage. Also, you need to demonstrate critical thinking.

Implement and follow up on the solution

You may need to convince the team about implementing the solution. When you involve the team from the beginning of the process, it leads to less resistance to the implementation phase. You must test the proposed solution to ensure you are satisfied; ensure no assumptions cause catastrophic outcomes. Record lessons learned and make necessary adjustments before going live. Furthermore, have a pilot system, especially when the full implementation involves multiple sites. It is easier to abandon or make necessary changes to one set up than to various locations. Exhibit leadership skills by championing the implementation process with effective communication to team members. Be clear about how you expect the team to deliver results. When a solution is implemented, follow up closely with continuous monitoring of actual events against expectations. Make room for final tweaks and adjustments to reach the finished article.

TIP: you need good project management skills to succeed at the implementation stage.

The most common pitfalls to problem-solving:

- neglecting to test/pilot and jumping straight to implementing stage.

- taking on sole responsibility for the problem and the solution, and not involving the team members and stakeholders at the early stages of the problem-solving process.

- jumping to an obvious solution without due consideration or evidence that it will work.

- failing to monitor and check that the problem has been solved.

Implement the problem-solving process to overcome challenges in your business.

Chapter 4: EFFECTIVE COMMUNICATION

"Be sincere; be brief; be seated."

— Franklin D. Roosevelt

What is communication?

There are many definitions of communication. The *Oxford Concise Dictionary* defines communication as: "the activity or process of expressing ideas and feelings or of giving people information." So, communication is certainly more than just words. Communication can be non-verbal, which can be transmitted through facial expressions, posture, hand gestures, and appearance.

Non-verbal communication portrays the speaker's subtle characteristics, such as sarcasm, complacency, and authenticity. You get a promotion: though you hear the word 'congratulations,' the body language suggests a lack of sincerity. Visual communication includes using signs, sketches, and colour, for example, to reinforce verbal communication.

To succeed in business or industry, you need to communicate effectively with superiors, colleagues, and staff in person and via email, social media, and mobile phone. Practical communication skills will land you promotions and aid your success in life. Here, we go through the communication skills you need to exhibit to succeed.

Listening

You have two ears and one mouth for a reason, so being a good listener is essential to becoming a good communicator. Good listening skills allow you to hear what is being said and to process the message. Good listening requires paying close attention and not unnecessarily interrupting the speaker. You will be amazed at what you can hear when you give your undivided attention to the message.

Non-verbal communication

You must pay attention to how you say the message, as well as body language, hand gestures, and eye contact that portray emotions. Equally, pay close attention to non-verbal signals when you communicate with others because it allows you to understand anything coded in the message.

Clarity and concision

There is a temptation to keep rambling on until you feel you are being heard. However, a good communicator must convey their message clearly and briefly without adding too much detail. People have short attention spans. So, writing unnecessarily long emails or messages may turn off your audience from reading to the very end and cause them to miss key points. Identify the purpose of sending your message and be definite, unambiguous, and concise.

Confidence

You need to be confident when communicating verbally, or through other mediums, with your work colleagues and subordinates. People will sense you are optimistic; they want to follow a confident leader with good ideas. Confidence in your communication attests to the listener or reader that you genuinely believe in what you are saying and follow through. Leaders and managers will be prepared to listen to confident employees.

Respect for others

You must respect that people will have different accents and must show people that you are paying attention to what they have to say. Take the time to spell people's names correctly and address people with correct and respectful salutations. Let people know that you are trying to hear their views. While you may agree to disagree, value their opinion.

Feedback

Take the opportunity to provide feedback that is constructive, with opportunities for improvement, and offer praise where due. Likewise, encourage people to give you feedback and evaluate ways to implement feedback where possible. Ask clarifying questions to make sure you have understood correctly.

Pick the right medium

Plan and prepare your message and identify how you want to send your message across. Ensure you choose a mode of communication that meets the required protocols and shows the right attitude.

Chapter 5: LEADERSHIP

"Leadership is not a position or a title; it is action and example."

— Donald McGannon.

A leader uses the art of inspiration to act and lead by example, with a strategy to achieve set company goals and objectives. Throughout history, many great leaders have emerged who have excelled in various facets of life. We can think of great founders such as Walt Disney, geniuses such as Albert Einstein, or reformers such as Dr Martin Luther King Jr. In every business and workplace, leaders are selected to inspire and direct actions to achieve company objectives. Every successful company relies on influential leaders to build and motivate teams to function well to achieve a common goal. Your ability to demonstrate good leadership skills will stand you in good stead in your career. Good leadership produces an inspiring environment. People want to work well for good leaders to achieve expected results, while ineffective leadership is a nightmare. A weak leader breeds bad morale and low productivity. To watch an ineffective leader is to see a cart lead the horse for a 100-mile journey. Even a one-mile trip is painful to watch. Some observers might say the end justifies the means, as long as you get to the destination. Still, there is a better way. The right leadership skills can help you in all aspects of your career, from climbing the corporate ladder to running your own business.

Leadership skills

In John C. Maxwell's book, *Leadership 101*, he makes this insightful observation about developing and growing as a leader: "Your leadership ability – for better or for worse – always determines your effectiveness and the potential impact of your organization." To start growing as a leader, you need to appreciate and understand a good leader's traits.

The following list is non-exhaustive, so use this as a starting point.

Discipline

Before you set out to change the world, you must first lead yourself very well. You must lead by example and be disciplined. Suppose you are typically five minutes late for meetings. How can you expect to correct your team member who is five days late in submitting monthly reports? You must have self-discipline if you imagine having discipline in your team. The business will have priorities. Focus on these, and do not get distracted. Evaluate business priorities regularly and ensure your team efforts are aligned to them.

Trust

You can rely on and trust good leaders because they keep their promises. A good leader develops a resilient team prepared to take appropriate and reasonable business risks. A dependable leader allows their team to be open about challenges and offers solutions to problems. A good leader is transparent with team members, accountable, and takes ownership of team actions.

Vision

A good leader articulates a vision well to the team. The team members know what is required and the goals that must be achieved. As a leader, you will learn to grapple with uncertainties. Still, your ability to articulate complex issues in simple, understandable terms will stand you in good stead. Team members will believe in you if they can see you believe in the vision and explain it well. A good leader with vision is decisive and improves project delivery and efficiency.

Problem-solving

The higher you go in your career ladder, the more problems you must solve. The main reason you are paid more is that you are expected to solve problems. A fair leader uses sound judgment to resolve issues that arise in projects and manoeuvres around obstacles. Problem-solving gets better with dipping into your experience to solve unknowns and avoid the undesired outcomes.

Teach and mentor

Leaders create and sell a vision. A good leader teaches team members to understand areas of complexity and improves individuals. A good leader mentors team members and puts a structure in place that encourages their personal development. A good leader empowers team members so they do not rely heavily on the leader to do their day-to-day jobs. Good leaders inspire team members to become high performers, and they are good role models. Mentoring includes encouraging others to be high performers. Mentoring also involves delegation to improve team members' confidence and to empower them to be high performers. A good leader takes time to give team members praise and feedback to build their morale.

Influence

Ultimately, to succeed as a leader, you must influence others, whether in your team or your line manager, suppliers, clients, or partners. Your ability to influence others is critical to being able to lead others. Influencing others is about making people want to do something and not asking them to do something because you have the authority or power to do so. There may be instances where you do not have the authority to make people do things, but instead, convince them and collaborate with them to achieve goals. For a leader to make an impact, they must positively influence others. A good leader positively influences others by focusing on what is in it for the other party and not just stating what they want.

Chapter 6: ADAPTABILITY

"And the most successful people are those who accept and adapt to constant change. This adaptability requires a degree of flexibility and humility most people can't manage."

— Paul Lutus

The *Oxford Concise Dictionary* defines adaptability as the quality of being able to change or be changed to deal successfully with new situations. The constant thing in business is change. Being adaptable means you respond very well to changing responsibilities, priorities, trends, expectations, and other work processes. Flexible people show that they are willing to learn new things and make necessary adjustments to suit transitions. At least every two or three years, you will see new captains or line managers joining your organization or setting up a relationship with new business partners. New kings have new laws, as they say. This becomes challenging when you are reluctant to change. Beware of specific team members who resist change. They see change as a pain they do not want, and so they push back at all costs. An adaptable person navigates around changing circumstances to achieve success by learning a new method and unlearning certain habits.

How to improve your adaptability skills

Practice the following to improve your adaptability skills.

Be aware of changes in your environment

Changes that happen in the workplace may be slow-paced such that you have to stay alert to recognize them. Life may not warn you of specific changes or the scale of them. So, you must be observant and remain conscious of changes in your business and work environment. Company policies change due to new legislation and best practice, so you need to be alert and have a method of tracking these changes to adapt accordingly. An adaptable person with a growth mindset knows that mistakes will be made in trying new things. Still, they work hard to avoid repeating mistakes and put checks and balances in place to minimize the impact of possible errors.

Develop a growth mindset

What brought you here will not necessarily take you there. If you have this mindset, you are prepared to grow by learning and applying new ideas. But not just learning new things; you must be willing to unlearn some old habits to help you seize new opportunities. Continuing to do what you always did will only let you have what you have always had. A growth mindset means you have the patience and resilience to continue to improve and are committed to overcoming challenges and obstacles. A growth mindset means that, while you are confident in your abilities, you are also open to improvements.

Be resourceful

Be adaptable to new situations. Know how to use existing resources and new techniques to achieve results. You may ask for and get new, unique resources; however, an adaptable person is creative at making use of existing resources to achieve new goals. A resourceful person learns from others and uses lessons to navigate change. An innovative person is willing to ask for tips and guidance from people inside and outside their organization and to adopt ideas for new ventures and opportunities. An adaptable, resourceful person knows how to ask the right questions to break the mould of established beliefs and move boundaries.

Chapter 7: CREATIVITY

"Creativity is inventing, experimenting, growing, taking risks, breaking rules, making mistakes, and having fun."

— Mary Lou Cook

The *Oxford Concise Dictionary* defines creativity as the use of skill and imagination to produce something new or to produce art. Creativity is putting curiosity and vision into action. Interest makes you ask why and why not. Imagination allows you to see it in existence and makes you think through all the possibilities. At the same time, creativity brings your curiosity and vision into reality. Creativity is unique, so know that it is more than likely that which you care to be curious about and dare to imagine but will mean absolutely nothing to others. So, do not take it personally when the fruits of creative works are overlooked or undermined. You have creative ideas for a reason. You will have to take responsibility to see it happen. It is good to seek feedback and support in turning your creative works into reality.

If you are a leader, you need your persuasion skills to convince the team and partners to come on board with your creative ideas. You must also understand creative ideas brought to you. Sometimes, you may have to park these ideas but be willing to revisit them if new opportunities to implement them emerge. Timing is vital for the implementation of creative ideas. When creativity leads to new ideas and products, then it is an invention. Creativity, though, does not have to begin with a blank sheet. Instead, you can make new connections between existing ideas and processes. So, through your thinking about the current process, you start to make new connections and permutations that have not been thought of before.

How to improve your creativity skills

Everyone is born creative. However, as we grow, some practice creativity more than others. It could be lying dormant for years, sometimes from as far back as early childhood. Everyone can practice being more creative to solve problems and offer solutions.

You will create some natural waste

You must permit yourself to produce results that will not be the finished article. It will take a lot of fine-tuning and thinking to get to the final piece. It can be like a buried diamond that must be unearthed and polished. Manage your expectations and frustrations in your quest to achieve the finished piece.

Create a schedule

Apportion regular time in your diary to attend to the piece of creative work. That way it does not matter whether you are in the mood to work on it or not; you turn up and make progress. Creating a schedule ensures you are not at the mercy of your whims to work on it or not.

Creativity is a process and not an act

To create something unique takes time. It does not have to take forever; however, you will not always achieve it in a single shot. Be patient to stick to the process. You must put emphasis on the process, not just the product, to make things happen.

Allow time to think and reflect

We live in a time where everything is rushed through to make money as soon as possible. Businesses that do not innovate fail to make time to reflect on creative ideas and opportunities. Do not fall into that trap; make time to ask authentic questions, and share your reflections. Do not rush or seek instant answers. Take time to think about your response and feedback.

Have a passion for what you do

It is best if you had a passion for what you do, as this will take you through the twists and turns of the creative process. You will struggle to go through the creative journey if your interest is limited and in short supply. When you set up a team to work on a creative project, be sure to pick those who have passion for the project or try to instill passion in the group.

Beware of the following:

Routine

Suppose everything you do is just going through the usual motions? In that case, your mind can fall into autopilot. You must spend time consciously thinking about the challenges and how to provide solutions.

We have always done it this way

This is particularly relevant if you work for an established and successful company. When you develop new ideas to provide solutions, be open to constructive criticisms and feedback to improve the process. However, beware of comments such as "We have always done it this way," or "We tried this ten years ago, and it didn't work." This mentality demonstrates opposition to new ideas. You must take the points of why it did not work ten years ago seriously; however, circumstances and situations change. Now could be the perfect time to resolve any issues and remove any barriers.

Chapter 8: ANALYSING INFORMATION

"Your relevance as a data custodian is your ability to analyze and interpret it. If you cannot, your replacement is due."

— Wisdom Kwashie Mensah

A long time ago, society disseminated information in a variety of formats in public libraries. Traditionally, many people also relied on the media and word of mouth for their information. The advent of computers and the worldwide web means data is available everywhere on different devices such as laptops, tablets, mobile phones, and desktop computers. You can type or talk to Alexa, Siri, or Google robots. To excel in your workplace or business, you need access to information to make informed decisions. Different forms of communication are available to you in the form of company policies, international and local standards, publications, journals, magazines, and many more. And of course, work colleagues pass on vital information which enables you to do your job. Take due diligence to make sure the information you have acquired is accurate. You are as good as the information on which you base your decisions.

How to analyse information

It is fair to say there has been an explosion of information available to everyone. The challenge is how to gather, manage, and analyse that information so you can make sense of it. To make quality decisions and provide sound judgment, you rely on accurate information.

Some tips for analyzing information

- It would be best if you determined the accuracy, relevance, and reliability of the information.

Gather detailed information from the source. If you wish to use data from an article, you must go to the source to check for reliability and consistency.

- Recognize interrelationships and themes. Take note of and explore any similarities. Review the information you have gathered to make sure there are no disparate pieces of information.

- Differentiate to find what is unique about the information. Check if there are any assumptions you need to verify.

Chapter 9: COACHABILITY

"My best skill was that I was coachable. I was a
sponge and aggressive to learn."

— Michael Jordan

A coachable person is capable of being easily taught
and trained to do something better. To succeed in life
and the workplace, you must be coachable. To be
coachable, you must pass two tests: you must be willing
to learn and have the willingness to accept change. A
coachable person wishes to grow, learn, improve, and
excel at what they do.

How to maintain being coachable

Ask for feedback

You must open the door to feedback. Someone who is coachable is open to feedback so that there is no tension from mentors and sponsors. Coachable people ask for feedback sincerely because they understand that they need it.

Show gratitude for receiving feedback

Most people give back because they genuinely love to help. And what goes around comes around. A sincere appreciation of the support you receive motivates the mentor or sponsor. Naturally, you feel like doing more when your efforts and time are appreciated. How you listen and pay attention to feedback is a critical non-verbal signal for showing gratitude.

Find a mentor and a sponsor

If you are in the early stages of your career, you need to find a mentor capable and willing to coach you in your formative years. However, if you are an experienced employee, you must get a sponsor that is willing to speak on your behalf and invest in your coaching and mentorship. If there is one magic bullet with a high probability of skyrocketing your career, it is finding a good sponsor. In Sylvia Ann Hewlett's book, *Find a Sponsor*, she puts forward that finding a sponsor is a new way to fast-track your career. Because a sponsor puts your hat in the ring for promotion, they have your back and speak about you when companies are looking for talent. Remember, in life, you must be in the race to win.

Show you are the right investment

A mentor or sponsor agrees to develop you to be ready to take on key responsibilities. You must grasp this opportunity and practice your newly-learnt skills in your regular meetings. Show the investment made in you is paying off to the benefit of the organization and society. You must have the self-discipline to show up on time for meetings and submit reports on time because these are all good indicators for your mentor. Take the time to research topics for discussions with mentors and sponsors; the quality of the questions you ask, and your views and opinions will demonstrate to them that they have invested their time and effort wisely with you.

Chapter 10: MENTAL HEALTH

"It's up to you today to start making healthy choices. Not choices that are just healthy for your body, but healthy for your mind."

— Steve Maraboli

According to the World Health Organization (WHO), mental health is "a state of wellbeing in which the individual realizes his or her abilities, can cope with the normal stresses of life, can work productively and fruitfully, and can contribute to his or her community." So, mental health refers to how people think, feel, and behave. Nonetheless, some people use the term "mental health" to imply disorder.

Why have I decided to choose mental health as one of the vital life skills young people need? Yes, mental health is not necessarily a skill as such, like the other nine chapters we discussed. Nonetheless, everyone needs good mental health to be able to fire on all cylinders in our livelihoods. Research by the United Kingdom National Health Service (www.england.nhs.uk/mental-health) indicates that "one in four adults and one in ten children experience mental illness during their lifetime, and many more of us know and care for people who do." Mental health affects people's lives and physical health, and vice versa.

From the WHO's definition, mental health is more than just avoiding functional mental disorders and disabilities; it's generating ongoing wellness and working fruitfully to contribute to society. To succeed in your workplace and your business, you must take active steps to look after your mental wellbeing. National Health Service England confirms that "improved mental health and wellbeing is associated with a range of better outcomes for people of all ages and backgrounds.

These include:

- improved physical health and life expectancy

- better educational achievement

- increased skills

- reduced health risk behaviours such as smoking and alcohol misuse

- reduced risk of mental health problems and suicide

- improved employment rates and productivity

- reduced anti-social behaviour and criminality

- and higher levels of social interaction and participation."

People have always had challenges and problems since the beginning of time. Today, the advent of the computer means that people can do more work now than ever before. The human brain is bombarded with a truckload of information which can sometimes overwhelm the mind. Most of the time, your brain is flooded with information until you sleep. Even at bedtime, it feels as if the brain is in overdrive. Suddenly, closing your eyes to sleep feels like pulling the handbrake while driving at 70 miles an hour on the motorway. Of course, that would be fatal, but that is how we expect our brains to cope with this emergency stop. It is difficult to imagine the harm caused to the mind by constant and excessive exposure to information.

In this chapter, so far, I have sought to emphasize why we need to pay attention to mental health. Now, I share some tips on how to maintain peak mental health so you can avoid dysfunctional conditions and improve productivity.

Tips for mental wellbeing

Connect with other people

Maintaining good relationships is an essential part of your mental wellbeing. Good relationships build a sense of belonging and self-worth. Humans are social animals that thrive on the emotional support of loved ones. Spend time with your loved ones, sharing experiences, and encouraging one another. Disconnect the TV and spend time with your children, friends, or family. Every quarter or so, I make it a habit to reach out to my old friends, sometimes as far back as high school classmates. The right relationships allow you to share good experiences and give you support through the bad.

Be physically active

Evidence shows that being active is not only good for your physical health and fitness, but it also improves your mental wellbeing. It causes chemical changes in your brain, which can positively change your mood. Set up a regular exercise routine in your schedule.

Identify your passion and learn new skills

Learn new skills around your hobby and interests to improve your mental wellbeing. Learning a new skill boosts your self-confidence, gives a sense of purpose, and helps you connect with others. If these new abilities are linked to your passions, you will find that you make time in your busy schedule to bring learning into your life. The new skill does not have to be about new qualifications or sitting exams, but rather about completing fun activities around your hobbies and interest.

Always protect yourself

Society has become ingrained to complain bitterly about the things you have not done or missed. These constant demands mean that we are mostly playing catch-up, and we cannot stop to live in the moment. These continuing demands push people to look to the future and remind them of their shortcomings yesterday. Take time to live in the present moment.

Be thankful daily

Spend five minutes daily to be thankful for what you have achieved, even if it is not what other people expected of you. You can work hard to get better results tomorrow but stop for a moment to be thankful. Someone, somewhere, is praying hard to get the job or status that you have and making the most of it. Some people must walk hours just to get decent drinking water and a light source, but you may be lucky enough to have these resources at the turn of a tap and flick of a switch. So, be thankful for the small things, as well as the big ones.

Meditate

Spend time to shut off from the outside world and allow the brain to cool off before you go to bed. You must make this conscious choice to find time in your busy schedules to meditate and stay still for a moment. If you are spiritual, you can pray while you meditate; if you are not, you can perform some yoga as part of your meditation.

Have moral courage

Unfortunately, in this world, there are bullies. And bullies thrive because good people look the other way and do not stand up to them. If you are being bullied in your workplace or elsewhere, have the moral courage to call out the bullies. Bullies pick on those they perceive to be weak. So, if they choose you, you need the moral courage to let them know they have got it wrong, and you will not put up with their bullying.

Likewise, if there is a bully at work or in society, do not look the other way just because you are not at the receiving end. Bullies will not flourish in a civilized environment where they are called out for their intolerable behaviour. But they will flourish in an environment where they know they will get away with it. Get a witness where possible and remind the bully that there are consequences to their actions, such as getting human resources and law enforcement involved.

Give back to society

Giving and kindness help your mental wellbeing because you get positive feelings of purpose and self-worth. This may not always be appreciated in the corporate world, but seeing the impact it can have when you give back to other people in your community is very rewarding.

Seek support when needed.

If you feel you are struggling to keep up with your mental wellbeing or have a mental illness, do not bottle it up. Someone is out there willing to listen to you, whether it's a family member or a medical professional. The earlier you discuss these potential issues, the better. Society is now more aware of mental health. There is less denial of the reality of mental health compared to decades ago.

A medical specialist is best placed to point you in the right direction for any further help. Do not wait too long to seek help because trained professionals will be pleased to assist in a confidential setting.

Conclusion

"Successful people are simply those with successful habits."

— Brian Tracy

These life skills have been shared to provide insight into the habits that allow us to have a successful career or run our business. The skills have been identified during my career experiences in various sectors such as from the manufacturing industry, the oil and gas industry, the military to academia.

These life skills are not a revelation, nor are they set in stone but rather reminders that generate results. They are based on my studies of the performances of work colleagues who have achieved success in their careers. They are intended to help you stand out early in your career and beat the competition for the best promotions and achievements in your workplace. Use them to positively impact your workplace and leave a lasting, positive impression so you can excel in your career or business.

This book is for those who dare to dream of advancing their career with improved remunerations, for example. To reach a higher echelon in your career, one must take calculated risks, resolve conflicts, deal with business problems, and provide solutions to meet company goals. Achieving these goals will come with disappointments and pain at times. One needs resilience to thrive and go through the process of attaining the expected outcome. A proactive leader prepares adequately for potential situations. To plan is to foresee what could happen and make available all the resources needed to deal with challenges. We inevitably cannot stop every future project challenges. However, leaders must frequently ask questions and seek feedback to make improvements and potentially save time.

One of the reasons managers could be paid more than the team members is that leaders can deal with problems and provide solutions. So, one's ability to use logic, imagination, and critical thinking to navigate the problem-solving process is crucial to succeeding in one's career. The lessons learnt from previous projects presents excellent opportunities to improve on future business endeavours. A leader who communicates clearly and concisely to their peers facilitates coordination and understanding within their teams. We reveal our competence and confidence whenever we communicate verbally and non-verbally. Poor communication in teams breeds misunderstanding and triggers frustration.

Regardless of the magnitude of the challenges at stake, a person with good leadership skills is fun to work with because they inspire everyone to achieve their utmost best. A good leader earns the team's trust because they articulate their vision excellently. They keep their promises and are open about challenges. The constant thing in life is change. The adaptable leader is conscious of changing; they manoeuvre around obstacles and use stumbling blocks as steppingstones. The versatile leader acknowledges that they would not have adequate resources all the time. Thus, they learn to modify existing resources or blend existing resources with new techniques to deliver expected outputs.

A creative person puts their curiosity and vision into action to deliver something new. Creativity involves exploring possibilities beyond the boundaries of existing rules and taking risks that could lead to failure. Nonetheless, a person with creative skills is patient with the creative process and uses feedback to improve the next iteration. The explosion of information available to businesses requires a person to gather, organise, and analyse data to provide a helpful context. A good information analysis allows a practical business problem synthesis and offers meaningful solutions.

To have a successful career, one needs to be willing to learn new ideas to grow and be outstanding at what they do. A coachable person succeeds in their job because they take ownership and accountability for their decisions and actions. Mentors can provide all the support needed; however, a mentee needs to show or prove that time invested in developing them is well worth it. Likewise, sponsors would like to put your hat in the ring to demonstrate you are a suitable investment. High-performing people have an excellent productivity rate per unit input of time. They can deliver results with minimum resources and are very efficient at what they do. To give a very high work rate requires one to be physical and mentally healthy. Maintaining mental health is less noticeable compared to physical health. Thus, we discussed mental health to highlight its impact on one's ability to work fruitfully and maintain consistent high performance at the highest level one aspires to be in their career.

If you are new to these personal skills, can it all be that easy? No, of course not. To exhibit these personal skills takes practice to improve. If it were all easy, everyone would do it effortlessly. Remember, it is not the strongest and the most intelligent that survives, but rather the most resilient and responsive to change. No doubt, some of the personal skills will come easy for you, and there are others that you may have to work hard to get better at. Practice perseverance as you respond to change and go through the process of personal growth to become a high-performing person.

Suppose you are in your career or business in the early years. In that case, you can use these critical skills as pointers for outstanding behaviours. You must strive to practice daily and at every opportunity. When you are assigned a project to deliver or work on as part of a team, it will help to look for ways to implement these skills. Because practising these skills will build your confidence and allow you to improve and get better at showcasing them. You will recognise that your improvements in exhibiting these skills reflect on your outputs.

Likewise, suppose you already have many years of work experience. In that case, you will use the ten personal skills as a reference guide to remind you of critical behaviours that, when exhibited, will help you stand out from your peers. Observe the habits of people who have excelled exceptionally throughout the years in your company. Look at how they present during team meetings and how they tackle project challenges.

You will see the clear signs that they are brilliant at exhibiting these critical life skills. It is never too late to learn and practice these personal skills to excel in your career.

When you have questions on any of the personal skills, take the opportunity to discuss with your mentor or sponsor. It would be helpful to keep in touch with your mentor or sponsor regularly. Seek continuous feedback from stakeholders such as line managers, team members, clients, and suppliers – and use that information to improve your skills. You cannot improve what you cannot measure. Use the feedback as a tool to identify what you can learn and improve.

About the Author

Enock A Ebbah is an engineering projects leader who currently lives in Coventry, United Kingdom. He has many years of experience working in the oil and gas industry, the British Army, academia, and the automotive manufacturing sectors.

In his spare time, he volunteers for youth charities in England and Wales. He enjoys working with young people to inspire and coach them to realize their potential.

Any feedback or questions?

Email me at <u>enock@ebbahsustainovation.co</u> or contact me on LinkedIn social network.

LinkedIn: <u>https://www.linkedin.com/in/enockaebbah/</u>